Data Analytics

*The Comprehensive Beginner's Guide to
Learn Data Analytics with Practical Data
Analytics and Statistical to empower and
evolve any business , using the power of
Data Analytics*

Owen Kriev

i

Table of contents

Chapter 1: Introduction

Data is a constantly changing and growing thing. A person contributes at least 100GB of data to this growth. Multiply that with the number of connected people around the world, data is continuously on the rise and with that comes a need for efficient data analytics.

Data analytics has helped companies in achieving a competitive advantage. It has helped them in becoming the leaders in their respective industries. Every year, businesses introduce a new and better way of doing different processes. With the help of expert data analysts, innovations are made possible. It all boils down to who among them is the quickest and who can create new ideas from all the data produced by people on the daily.

What is data analytics?

Data analytics is the science of analyzing raw data when it comes to extracting useful information. Companies would then use this to help improve the way they run things; this can influence how their system works or how they interact with their clientele. Data analytics allows people to make better decisions, to refute existing theories, and to replace these theories with more factual ones.

Data analytics involves the process of gathering data and testing results to look for correlations between the values of a data set. Once this has been accomplished, the collected result is then used to formulate new theories—usually, ones which improves on the previous ones. With the growth of raw unused and untapped data, many industries are investing in studies despite the shortage of data analysts.

The primary components in data analytics include:

- *The management*
- *The data analyst*
- *The data sources*

These three basic components of data analytics are essential when it comes to completing the process.

With the ever-changing ways of data gathering, some of the techniques may vary but the way of analyzing data remains the same. You would need statistical skills, technical knowledge, and business knowledge to perform the job. Without these essential skill sets, it would be difficult for a person to proceed. In some cases, knowledge in programming would also necessary when you are dealing with a data set that requires complex statistical computations.

In this book, we will:

Discuss the different topics that are integral to data analytics. Here, you'll learn more about the basics that should provide you with ample information when proceeding in this field.

Chapter 2: Overview of Data Analytics

Data analytics can help your business when it comes to gaining an advantage over their existing competition. Competitive advantage is providing value to stakeholders by developing better customer service and enhancing business operations. Even new businesses can benefit from this—but to do so, you must learn how to make proper use of it. Having the data is one thing, but knowing how to assess and what to do with it is another.

Different Applications of Data Analytics:

The travel and gaming industry, healthcare and medical institutions, as well as the energy corporations are the industries that benefit most from data analytics. Other business companies use the principles of data analytics to improve their operation's efficiency. This includes: *market optimization, better people management and improving network security.*

I.   Market Optimization and Segmentation:

The most common purpose of data analytics would be for optimizing market campaigns, and taking market data in order to enhance the company's services and/or products.

Businesses evolve from a creative process into a data-driven process of formulating marketing strategies. Nowadays, marketing professionals and organizations use data analytics to identify the possible outcomes of marketing campaigns and to make sound decisions in targeting specific customers.

A data analyst uses conjoint analysis and demographic studies to optimize marketing strategies and to create proper market segmentation. Data sources may come from social media information, online surveys and other web related resources to analyze a specific market. Conjoint analysis uses online surveys to gather data.

A good example of data analytics is Google Analytics. This tool is free and enables marketers to collect information on the behavior of people while browsing the web. With this kind of data analytics, a marketer can improve details such as the wording of a campaign, or develop a landing page that convinces people to click.

II.   Risk Reduction:

Businesses engage in investing activities every day. These investments increase the overall income of a business and as such, proper investment management is crucial. With data analytics, an analyst can evaluate the different risks involved with an investment. Using various investment data sources, an analyst can make proper recommendations on how to minimize risks and how to diversify investment portfolios appropriately.

III.   People Management:

Data analytics has helped many businesses manage their human resources. The purpose of data analytics in managing people is to determine potential employees from the many applicants, to identify employees who deserve an award or promotion and to describe job designations with proper responsibilities.

With data analytics, an analyst can use categorical variables to determine the specific characteristics of an excellent and top-performing employee. A data analyst can also make use of a dataset on benefits and payroll administration from external sources in recommending the best benefits to encourage employee's loyalty and commitment.

IV. Evaluation of Loan Portfolios and the Involved Risk:

Banks and lending institutions use data analytics to determine and evaluate the risk of a loan portfolio. With time series analysis, a data analyst can create a model that maximizes return and minimizes the risk of uncollectibles. Aside from determining when and who to lend money to, data analytics is also helpful in establishing the appropriate credit scores.

Credit scores can predict a person's behavior when it comes to insolvency. With these scores, lending institutions can evaluate an individual's credit worthiness. Insurance companies can also benefit from data analytics. Data analytics help them determine people who will likely avail of insurance and the possibilities that a policyholder will claim insurance.

Digital Applications:

The most common application of digital data analytics can be seen in search engine optimization. Businesses use digital data to optimize their e-commerce sites. An analyst can transform digital data into reports that help businesses achieve a digital edge in terms of optimizations and automation of business processes.

Another common application of digital data analytics is software evaluation, wherein the analyst can evaluate digital data to identify software usage and behavior. Using this data, a business can further improve their existing applications or develop a new one to cater the needs of their customers.

I.   **Improving Safety and Security:**

With data analytics, IT and data analytics professionals can gather security issues and analyze these data to understand events that create risk and security breach to the business' network. Through these analyses, a data analyst can recommend extensive security measures to the business.

Foundations of Data Analytics

The success of data analytics depends on building the right foundation for each process performed. A good foundation aids a data analyst in utilizing the full power of data analytics. Without a strong foundation, the business can end up wasting valuable resources for research.

I.   **Data Analytics Team:**

In a larger scope of data analytics, a team consists of seven key roles. Each role contributes to the success of data analytics. These roles are:

- Business users
- Project sponsor
- Business intelligence analyst
- Database administrator
- Data engineer

- Data scientist.

In a small to a medium scale business setting, the business users, business intelligence or data analyst and database administrator are enough to complete a data analytics project. The business users refer to the management, executive officers, and senior executives of a company who are seeking for ways to solve an existing problem in the business.

A business intelligence or data analyst must possess the right skill sets such as technical knowledge and business knowledge. This person should also have an extensive knowledge of the use of data machines and machine learning to complete complex tasks such as programming and computations.

A database administrator provides the necessary data sources if an internal database is needed during the study. Oftentimes, this key role is unnecessary if the data analytics only involves survey study. The database administrator role becomes essential only during the implementation phase wherein certain changes on the business database are needed to reflect these changes.

The team works together to achieve the ultimate goal of properly analyzing collected data. Collaboration and communication are crucial. Every member of the team must communicate with each other in every phase of the project.

II.   Goal Identification:

The first phase of data analytics is identifying the goals of the study. The team brainstorms regarding the goals, the timeline in which they must achieve the results and the manner of communicating the insights. The business users should identify specific goals because this serves as the starting point of data analysis. Clearly defined goals help the data analyst in determining the type of study, and in aiding the database administrator procures the necessary data sources.

III.   Data and Data Preparation:

It begins with properly identifying the type of data and study required for the project. After this, the analyst begins to gather and prepare the data. Data gathering includes sending out surveys and questionnaires through online and offline channels. Alternatively, it entails formulating a hypothesis to test. During data preparation, data set are filtered with missing values, duplicate entries and outliers to minimize error in conclusions.

IV.   Data Analytics Process:

Data analytics can never succeed without a systematic process. The process includes data preparation, the creation of models and observation of data patterns and development of predictions. The results of data analytics are data insights. The data analyst must communicate these insights in a timely and effective manner.

V.   Tools and Techniques:

Statistical computations, regression analysis, standard deviation, business intelligence solutions, and analytics models are some of the tools you would need in data analytics. Each tool contributes to the completion of a data analytics project. The tools and techniques needed for data analytics depend on the input and the desired output of the study.

Getting Started:

A data analyst gathers and analyzes data based on the objectives of the research. They would make use of different methodologies to examine and explore a dataset. After exploration and evaluation of data and data patterns, they will communicate what they have learned and make recommendations accordingly. The processes involved in data analytics require the right skill sets to achieve results.

The Roles of a Data Analyst:

The biggest role of a data analyst is analyzing data. Analyzing data means finding useful patterns for decision making. In most cases, you deal with real-time data sources and historical data. During the analysis, you might work with IT professionals, database administrator, marketing department, and especially the boss.

Another role of a data analyst is being the planner of the study. You create the study plan. You recommend the proper data gathering processes. The last important role of a data analyst is being the reporter. Communicating the results to the upper management or to the users of the study is the ultimate goal of data analytics.

Data analytics would be rendered useless if they cannot provide a proper report or are unable to finish it. Even if the results are negative, communication is still required. Much like presenting an idea, these reports will come with visual aids in order to fully express the results of the study—clarity and simplicity is key.

The Different Skills of a Data Analyst

Data analyst deals with different data sources and communicates with various people. As a data analyst, you must possess the necessary skills in achieving results and in carrying out your responsibilities during a data analytics project.

1. Industry Knowledge – Knowing how a business operates is essential in data analytics. The management may orient you about the vision, mission, and goals of the company towards growth and success. However, the duty to obtain an in-depth study of a business and its processes is the responsibility of the data analyst.

    An internal study of the business involves any historical changes within the company. These historical changes may include understanding how the business uses data and other complex systems. You should also know when the business adopted an automated data system gathering. Discovery of any problems regarding data accumulation is also part of your job.

    External factors and competition study are important. The external factors help a data analyst understand how a business is able to thrive in its industry and how it handles competition. In a fast moving industry where innovations are the "thing" of the competition, fast results with a data analytics are required.

2. Problem Solving and Analytical Skills – Data analytics also involve using mathematics and statistics. In a data analytics project, you use many probability measures, as well as measures of central tendency which includes: mean, median, and mode, charts and graphs. These mathematical and statistical methods are just a few of the

many measures you should know. An extensive knowledge of these measures is advantageous in completing the job of a data analyst.

Coupled with expertise in mathematics and applied mathematics, you need analytical skills to interpret the results of the many equations and formulas to compute mean, deviation and other statistical computations. Ability to analyze large data while maintaining a keen attention to details is a great combination of an analytical mind. This is something you should develop.

Problem-solving skills entail analyzing a worded problem that business users want you to solve. Most of the times, the problems are so vague that you provide 80% of the given variables to solve the problem.

3. Technical Skills – These skills include programming and machine learning. Some companies require their data analyst to have a basic knowledge on Python and R language due to the statistical nature of data analytics. An advanced knowledge of machine learning such as MS Excel and other simple programs to analyze statistical variables is sufficient to finish a simple to a slightly complex study.

   Programming is not only limited to knowing computer languages such as R but also the knowledge to create and combine complex Excel functions to obtain results of a median, covariance and other statistical computations.

4. Efficient Business Skills – Data analytics involves planning the study and gathering data. In order to obtain good data source for your study, you should possess the skills of business people who know what to plan, how to plan, when, and how to execute a plan. The ability to ask the right questions is a fundamental business skill you will need to perform experiments and surveys.

5. Effective Communication skills – Written or oral communication skills include saying the right thing and presenting the results in a clear and concise manner. You need effective communication skills to be able to properly explain the results to the management or users of your study.

   Most managers or executive directors do not accept results written entirely in numbers. They want actionable results. Saying to them, "the company's sales revenue increases by 10% every year", is not enough. These managers want to know why and you should be able to provide them with concise answers based on facts. Keep in mind that your answer will also determine the changes they might end up making based upon your study.

   For example, you presented that the increase in sales every year is due to the new machine acquired by the company. Based on your study, the correlation between buying a new machine and sales increase is strong enough to warrant buying another new machine. The managers either decide to buy another new machine or tell you to make a further study. This study includes predicting the new machine's effect on the sales revenue of the company.

6. Mathematics and Analytics – Mathematics, particularly applied mathematics, is important in data analytics. This field helps a data analyst become a critical and a logical thinker. Results are not based on intuition alone but include data, numbers and formulas.

Distinction between mathematics and analytics:

Mathematics and data analytics are two different fields of study. Mathematics is the study of logic, quantity, and arrangement. Oftentimes, you use mathematics to explain why one variable affects the behavior of another variable.

Data analytics, on the other hand, involves the study of patterns and behavior in a dataset. You use mathematics to prove the existence of these patterns, to formulate a rationale for a new hypothesis and to create strategies to implement new models. Mathematics helps you solve a problem while data analytics aids you in creating a problem and solving this problem with mathematics.

Analysis and Analytics:

Many people use analysis and analytics interchangeably. Although these two involve analyzing data and using the results to improve a business operation, data analysis and data analytics are two different fields.

The major difference between data analysis and data analytics is the kind of data and the use of this data. Data analysis deals with past data sources. From the results of analyzing past data, the data analyst or the managers formulate recommendations.

A data analytics predicts the future behavior of a past data source. Using a past data source, the data analyst creates a model that predicts what will happen if a certain trend continues. Sometimes, a data analyst creates "predictions" based on real-time data sources.

The Scope of Study

In data analysis, an analyst uses a single data source. From this data source, he/she "dissects" the event into smaller parts to address the issues raised. For example, the management wants to learn the whys and whats in a sales report for the month of December. In order to answer the questions, the analyst gathers the data in that particular month. He/she must answer questions like the following:

–   Why did the company get a high figure in sales?
–   What did the company do to achieve such sales figures?
–   Who were the customers to come up with those sales figures?

As you can see, data analysis only attempts to answer what happened in the past on that particular month and with that specific sales figure.

Data analytics uses a wider scope of the study. Moreover, it includes data analysis to forecast what happens to the data. Data analytics is predictive in nature. More importantly, data analytics involve cleaning the data, eliminating missing values, and disregarding duplicate variables to come up with results. Data analytics uses applied mathematics and programming languages in creating a system to predict customer behavior or process outcomes.

Data analysis does not involve such extensive study. It ends in dissecting the data and making the decisions after the breaking down the dataset. Data analytics starts where data analysis ends. Using the "dissected" data, data analytics proceeds in creating a model for future use.

I.   *Micro vs. Macro*

Data analysis breaks down the micro components of a dataset. Using these components, the analyst would be able to come up with a conclusion based on a standard set by the company. Data analytics starts where data analysis stops. From micro components, data analytics steps up the study into a macro level, aggregating the micro-components to build models for forecast purposes.

Despite these major differences, data analysis and data analytics are two great tools in the business. Both methods are useful in improving business, in creating effective campaigns and other business applications. When combined, these two methods can boost a business' competency level significantly. However, it also depends on how well the analyst can communicate their data insight.

What Are Data Insights?

Data insights are valuable results derived from data analytics. Other terms may include output, outcome, forecast, and predictions. With data insights, the users can make informed decisions.

In digital applications of data analytics, valuable insights may mean engagement between the company and their clientele—comments, reviews all fall under this. An e-commerce site can determine the reasons why customers are not purchasing a particular product or are not staying long on the website. Insights help marketers identify the reasons a marketing campaign fails or succeeds.

A data analyst should know how to communicate these insights so business owners can apply these insights and improve on the areas they are lacking in. One way of communicating and representing data insights is data visualization tools. The use of graphs and charts is an example. A descriptive presentation is an effective method of communicating data insights.

You can use automated data services to perform the different tasks in data analytics and data insights communication. These services help you finish a data analytics project fast and allows you to proceed with the next project. With automated data services such business intelligence solutions, you can perform data analytics project simultaneously.

I. *Automated Data Services*

Data sources are assets to any organization. Turning these data sources into useful information is even more valuable. Businesses, government institutions, and educational organizations know how valuable data is in competition, in providing public services and in giving quality education.

However, few organizations have the capability for maximizing the benefits of big data analytics. Accurate data is hard to obtain. The speed and the complexity of data analytics prevent most organizations in utilizing the full potential of data and data analytics.

Even though there are a few companies and organizations manage to implement data analytics, the results of data analytics become useless because of certain disconnection from actual operations. With cloud computing platforms, organizations can combine data from all sources without spending so much and using up too many resources.

These automated services enable a data analyst to deliver a verifiable return on investment. The emergence of the internet and mobile technology changes the standard way of doing data analytics. Cloud computing makes it possible for organizations to exploit big data and use data analytics to extract useful information that can improve the operations of the organization. Although maintenance of cloud computing platforms is a little complex, its benefits surpass such disadvantage.

II.   The BENEFITS:

–   Strong Data Source: Reliability of data sources is an issue in data analytics. Results are not precise if the data source is incomplete, distributed and out-of-date. Many of the data sources are in the cloud. With cloud computing platforms, you can exploit the data sources found in the cloud. Cleaning, matching and merging these data sets with company objectives become easier because you have access to real-time data.

–   Enhanced teamwork: A cloud-based data management helps companies with teams found around the globe. Sharing of insights, models, and other data analytics fundamentals are easier than traditional data analytics. With cloud computing data analytics, team members can access other team members' work and results. They can use it to the existing system. As a result, business operations improve.

–   Scalability: A cloud-computing platform enables you to scale back and forth using the platform's analytics resources. If your operation changes, you can always go back, evaluate your previous results and apply it to your current data sources. If your business grows, you can expand the platform's resources to accommodate the change in resources and operation. You can change your analytics methods from simple to complex, and from complex to simple with ease.

- Cost Efficient: Traditional or on-premise data analytics requires updates to a newer version so that a business can use complex computations and methods. With a cloud-based platform, updates are ready. You do not need to install newer versions. Furthermore, automated data management and analytics require minimum IT intervention. You can use new features without spending big money on these features.

- Benefits of Data analytics for corporations: Every day, companies face challenges and pressure to maintain quality services and understand their customers. With data analytics and cloud computing platform, organizations can become competitive and can anticipate customer needs and wants. In this era where people share information in a relaxed manner, it is up to the companies to combine traditional and cloud computing methods to gather data and use this data.

Another benefit of data analytics and cloud computing would be ***products and services innovation***. Products and services are the essence of why an organization exists. Using data analytics, a company can create a new product that customer needs and may want to buy despite a lack of need to satisfy.

Innovation does not only mean the introduction of new products and services. It may also mean personalization. Every minute, customers use digital technologies, whether to share information or to avail of services. With data analytics and cloud computing, a company can personalize the experience of customers in using applications and service. An example of personalization is providing an interactive map when searching for restaurants or retail stores.

Benefits of Data Analytics for Government Use:

Private companies are not the only organizations that can benefit when it comes to using data analytics and cloud computing platforms. The government is the number one user of data analytics. One of the major benefits is preventing fraud. With the prevention of fraud, the government can increase revenues. How do they do that? By gathering data through cloud computing, the government would be obtain data on how much a person really earns. The government can also use it to track and mandate a taxpayer to pay the real tax due.

The second benefit of data analytics for government use would be enhancing the welfare of the citizens. An example is when government agencies use data to analyze information for pensioners within a particular state. With data analytics, these agencies can create strategies to convince pensioners to look for living quarters with a lower cost of maintenance without sacrificing comfort.

Aside from welfare enhancement, the public sector can also make use of data analytics and cloud computing to ensure public safety. The government data analyst can identify areas which are prone to fire and determine the causes of the fire. With this data, they can create strategies to increase awareness and a map to increase response time when a citizen calls for a fire emergency.

Another application of data analytics related to public safety is helping the police department make informed decisions when solving a crime. As a result, public confidence increases and crime unsolved decreases.

Benefits of Data Analytics for Academia:

Data analytics can help school administrators in creating a unified curriculum for the students, in identifying the degrees those incoming freshmen will likely to take and offering new courses to these students. Data analytics also enables schools and colleges in formulating scholarship strategies for its students, helping them graduate and find work.

Data Analytics is an excellent tool for analyzing data, whether it be big-scale or small-scale. It has so many applications and any organization can use data analytics for whatever purposes. Data analytics involve a process of gathering data, cleaning this data and testing it for results as per organization's goals.

Chapter 3: The Basics of Data Analytics

The foundation of data analytics is, of course, data. There's plenty available and different means of gathering new ones whenever needed. However, that isn't the only thing you need for data analytics. It also involves planning a study, establishing the types of gathering data and identifying the methods to select a sample.

I.   Planning a study

Data analytics start with defining a problem to solve. This problem does not necessarily mean a conflict in the business. The problem could refer to defining a new business objective such as increasing sales, improving operations and encouraging employees to stay by offering excellent benefits.

A practical application of defining a new and specific business objectives is to create a new system that predicts the insolvency behavior of new customers or to develop a credit score that rates customers and classify these customers into certain categories.

You can use the principle of a cross-industry standard process for data mining (CRISP-DM) to plan a study for your business. Oftentimes, a data analyst does not need to follow these stages in strict order. However, establishing a definite time frame for each stage is an advantage.

Strictly follow the time frame because data may become outdated or useless for exploration if they are left stagnant for a long period of time. Data is collected every day, every minute and every second. With each minute that passes, unused data for the data analytics means an opportunity lost.

II.   Setting up Business Goals

The major element of planning a study is determining specific business goals. This would determine why there is a need for the study. In this phase, the management should be specific about the business objectives for data analytics.

The reasons behind conducting a study must be reasonable. A vague objective is like working blindfolded. You would not know where to begin even if you have an idea how to begin.

Part of this stage is establishing the budget. Data analytics study entails resources. It means spending a certain amount of money and dedicating time to complete a project.

Although you can use your resourcefulness to minimize the cost of spending, you still need a start-up budget to begin the study. Communicate to the management how much do you need for a study to solve the problem. Sometimes, the management may solicit project sponsors to fund a data analytics research.

Remember, that one key role of a data analytics includes a project sponsor. If the management is planning for a big leap in innovating, project sponsors may become part of your data analytics team.

Aside from the management and business users, you will need to include the project sponsors when formulating the study plan. You need to identify what types of data you should be reporting to these people and how much information should be given to them.

III.   Gathering Data Records

Data analytics requires performing various activities. The first activity in this phase is the selection of the data set relevant to the business goal identified. This activity involves gathering different data sets—there are many methods you can use for this.

Remember, you are dealing with datasets that contain many variables or worst fuzzy data. Specific determination of goals cuts down the time spent in data selection. This means, you can dedicate more time in analyzing and building the appropriate data gathering tools and methods.

Although all stages are equally essential, time spent on selecting and gathering data should be short. If time on data gathering is short, the business saves resources in terms of money, manpower and effort.

IV.   Preparing and Exploring the Data

This involves cleaning the data, removing any outliers or filling in missing values. After cleaning the data, you need to explore the data. Data exploration involves testing the hypothesis if you are using experimentation method. It also includes using statistical models such as regression method, and standard deviation to establish concrete correlation between the variables.

V.   Reporting Data Insights

The last stage is communicating your completed data insights. You have to plan what type of charts to use when presenting your data results to the management and to the project sponsors if you are working with a large scale project. You can use a combination of descriptive and quantitative reporting.

There are times wherein the results may not be up to the standard of the management. If the management or the project sponsor wants a revision of the study, be ready to communicate and ask the type of changes to the study. Ask for proper evaluation so you know what part of the study to change.

Performance evaluation of the study is important. Failing once is okay but a repeat failure in data analytics is not practical. Failure of study means you are wasting precious resources. It means changing the data sources to match the needs of the management for decision making.

Methods for Gathering Datasets:

I.   Surveys

Surveys are data gathering tools that would collect information from people about their behavior, opinion, and comments on a specific topic. This method uses questions and is a type of a descriptive research.

Businesses used surveys because of its convenience. You can use online surveys, emails or the traditional way to gather data from participants. You can use surveys on feasibility studies for new businesses, on getting a general knowledge whether an idea will succeed or on evaluating past events.

  – **PROS**
A survey is convenient and easy to use. You can gather a large amount of data in just a few days or more. You can use different modes of communication to conduct a survey. You

can interview the participants, ask them questions through the phone or send your survey questions through email. The costs of conducting a survey are minimal.

– CONS

One common issue when it comes to using surveys is the construction of questions and choices. If you do not carefully plan and think of the questions to ask, you end up gathering data source that does not answer the problem of the study. Worst, you might create the wrong solutions. Most of the times, choices to the questions do not reflect the opinions of your participants.

The second issue is the response rate. Since a survey uses a sampling method, the data set might create biased results. Response rates may also not be enough to draw conclusions regarding the problem being solved. Respondents might not be the "true" participants of your study.

The third issue is the response of the participants. Participants might respond in a biased manner. For example, you want to know the general opinion of people regarding their spending behavior with credit cards. The respondents may answer they are using credit cards when in real life they do not even possess a card.

Another issue is the inability of surveys to follow trends in real time. You cannot measure changes between two time periods. Even though surveys are cheap, conducting another survey to know any changes in opinion or behavior is too expensive and time-consuming.

Furthermore, surveys cannot clearly define the cause and effect. Since you are gathering data on specific behaviors of a certain event in a limited time, determining causal relationship is difficult. You cannot establish that the effect arises because of the cause.

Lastly, access to the real population for your survey may be difficult to achieve. If you are using online channels to gather data, you might not obtain the necessary sampling size to make a survey a good source.

Example of a Survey

Here is sample of survey based on a template from https://www.surveymonkey.com. This template is a survey on customer satisfaction. It has ten questions with four or more multiple choices.

1. Please rate the likelihood of recommending our company and product to other people.

   0   1   2   3   4   5   6   7   8   9   10

2. Please rate your disappointment or satisfaction with our products/services and our company.

   - o   Satisfaction is guaranteed.
   - o   I am quite satisfied
   - o   Not really pleased nor dissatisfied
   - o   Slightly dissatisfied
   - o   I am very disappointed

3. Kindly choose the appropriate descriptions of our product. Choose all that applies.

   - o   Consistent
   - o   Superior quality
   - o   Helpful
   - o   Innovative
   - o   Affordable
   - o   Expensive

o Useless
o Ineffective
o Low quality
o Defective

4. Is our product helpful to you?

o Yes
o No

5. Please evaluate our product's quality.

o Very Superior quality
o Superior Quality
o Neither superior nor low quality
o Poor quality
o Very poor Quality

6. Please evaluate the reasonability of the price our products.

o Expensive
o Above Mid-range
o Mid-range
o Affordable
o Very Affordable

7. Please rate the responsiveness of our customer representatives on your questions and complaints on our products.

o Extremely approachable and responsive
o Very approachable and responsive
o Somewhat approachable and responsive
o Not so approachable and responsive
o Not approachable and responsive

8. Please tell us whether you are a longtime customer or a first-time buyer.

- o I am a first-time buyer
- o I've been a customer for 6 months
- o I've been buying products from the company for a year
- o I've been a customer for almost 2 years
- o I've been a customer for more than 2 years
- o I have not made a purchase yet.

9. Are you going to buy any of our products?

- o Yes, I will buy any of the products
- o It depends
- o No, I will not buy any of the products

10. Please leave comments, questions or concerns.

II.   Experiments

An experiment means testing a hypothesis. Generally, experiments are done to prove a scientific theory. However, you can use the principles of experiments to test a new theory and make recommendations based on the results of the testing.

– Basics of Experiments

One fundamental concept of an experiment is observation. You gather information from the subjects and establish the patterns of behavior using statistical computations.

You can use data observation or actual inspection of events, depending on what type of experimentation you are dealing with. Data observation involves looking for correlations between the variables of a historical dataset. Actual inspection of events is studying real-time processes.

The second fundamental is the creation of hypothesis. This is the main purpose of the study. Without the hypothesis, you cannot perform experimentation. Use the hypothesis to lead you when it comes to conducting multiple tests and produce an output.

The final concept is the result. The test should yield a result, whether it be positive or negative—this result becomes the basis of your recommendations. Your recommendations are the basis for management decision making.

– Types of Experiments:

There are two classifications of experiments. The first classification is the natural experiments. You formulate a theory based on observing a system without making any changes to the system.

The second classification is the controlled experiment. All variables are the same except for one. You change that independent variable and see how the other variables behave. You obtain the results and make conclusions. Manufacturing industry and pharmaceutical companies usually administer this kind of research.

– Uses of Experimentation in Business

Experimentation helps business in determining the behavior of their consumers. For example, a retail store creates two types of advertisement and commissions a TV to air these advertisements in two different time slots. The retail store wants to determine how viewers react to these advertisements.

Business industries experiment to meet the needs of their customers, and to match the ever increasing demand of people for new products and services. Experimentation is a big chunk of a business' fixed expense annually. An example of a business that uses experimentation a lot is the **telecommunications industry**. Innovation is what keeps them ahead of the competition. Those companies that do not give priority to research and development cannot keep up with the aggressive competition.

– Benefits of Experimentation

With experimentation, businesses can actually save on their resources. Before fully engaging their products to a new market, businesses test their theories on a limited market at a limited time. It lets businesses assess which products yield the best result and have this particular product enter the market with little risk of losing. Experimentation helps them determine the reactions of their target customers.

One of the challenges that businesses face is interpreting the results of experimentation. Sometimes, declaring a failed experiment or a successful one is difficult to do, especially for those businesses that are new to the use of experimentation. Another challenge is the issue of the sampling of the new market. The result isn't always 100% accurate.

When to use experimentation?

Experimentation provides a certain level of perception on what really works. Theoretically, it is easy to know which variation makes sense and leads to favorable results. Practically, it is near to impossible. Experimentation is often unnecessary in a small scale setting.

One thing to remember with experimentation is that the ultimate success depends on the execution of the information derived from the testing, not the hypothesis creation. The industry does not matter. The most successful insights are based on the possible impact and the value of strategic changes.

For example, a web store decided to change its website design. The theory is that this new design and arrangement can help increase customer engagement and convince customer to purchase. With experimentation, the analyst can test this theory really affects a reader's click-through or a consumer's bounce rate.

Alternatively, the analyst can conclude without any testing that the new design will generate more leads when compared to the old design. If the web store is a small scale business, it can launch the new design without testing its hypothesis. The analyst can back up the hypothesis with data observation and results from web stores who are using a similar design.

In conclusion, use experimentation if you are dealing with a large scale research. Experimentation is best when you know that the opportunity cost is higher than the cost of doing the study and that the business needs a scientific basis for backing up decisions.

How do you perform experiments in data analytics?

Designing a smart plan is crucial to the success of experimentation. Every day, a business management thinks of ways to improve operation, to enhance customer services and to introduce innovative products and services.

Many of these businesses implement new ideas without any concrete evidence to back up their decisions. As the data analyst of a business, the success of experimentation depends on how excellent the design of the study. It is your responsibility to ensure that the management does not fail with their decisions.

I.   Orienting People to the Process

The first part of experimentation is to orient managers and other people involved. The managers, project sponsors and business users should have an idea on how the experimentation is done.

Even if the process is easy to understand, communication remains an essential component. Sharing the knowledge of what composes a valid testing process makes the experimentation clearer and more specific. The data analyst knows what to deliver and the managers, business users and project sponsors know what to demand.

Orientation can begin with a simple brainstorming of all the people involved, from the senior executives or managers to the data analyst. Part of the orientation is gathering any potential hypothesis for the study.

II.   Creating a Testable Theory

Base the hypothesis on the existing operations of an organization or on an entirely new ground where no historical data exists. The first basis entails spending little on resources since you are using existing data set and existing customer base to gather data.

The second basis involves the creation of a hypothetical dataset and entails more resources. The risk of spending is higher than the first basis since you will be dealing with an untried dataset.

Both scenarios are testable but one scenario may not be feasible and may yield useless results to the management. In the end, the scenario that yields useless results cannot be considered testable in the context of experimentation because of its failure to bring useful information.

III.   Gathering Data

Gathering data starts with identifying the objective for the study. The study should answer the question: *What does the management want?* After objective identification, you determine the tool for gathering data and the sample size. There are many ways of gathering data. You can collect information through surveys or use an existing dataset from the management.

–   Using Surveys

The first step is formulating a survey, one that appeals to many in order to increase response rates from respondents. Then, tally the results. If you are using online survey tools to gather data, tallying is not necessary. The survey company where you availed the online survey will usually provide the tally results themselves. Use this tally results to explore the data and eliminate errors.

– Using Experimentation

If you are using experimentation, identify the type of data set to collect. This dataset can come from internal or external sources. Hypothesis formulation is necessary for this data gathering to work.

IV.   Data Exploration and Preparation

The first step in data exploration is identifying the input and output variables or the dependent and independent variables. Then, determine the categories and type of data. Are the data continuous, ordinal or nominal?

Before you can use the dataset for evaluation and hypothesis testing, you need to eliminate outliers, missing values, and errors. These biases in the dataset distort the results and may yield incorrect conclusions. After removing the errors and missing values, the next step is to use statistical methods such as mean, mode, regression analysis and other techniques to identify a correlation between the variables.

V.   Selecting a Useful Sample

Data gathering is costly and takes time. Most of the time, data is often unavailable. Even if data is unavailable, studying a whole population of a dataset is impractical. You would be dealing with a large amount of data if you are going to gather every variable and value. But, if you are working with a small scale business, getting a whole population is okay.

In place of a whole population, you can make use of sampling. Although a sample population consists of a small percentage of the whole dataset, you can still draw sound conclusions and make useful recommendations. The success of sampling depends on choosing the appropriate sampling method.

Choosing the right method means knowing the type of study you are performing. The types of study were discussed in the first part of this chapter. You can use four sampling strategies. These methods are random sampling, systematic sampling, and stratified random and rational sub-grouping.

– Random Sampling

Random sampling is useful when it comes to getting samples from a batch or historical data. Each value in the data set has an equal chance of being selected as part of the sample. This eliminates bias during the sampling process.

The process is simple. For example, you have a data population of 10,000 customers. In your research, you want a sample of 10% of the total population. The sample size is 1,000 customers. To select the 1,000 customers, assign each customer a number. The assigned number should be equivalent to the total size of the population, which is from 1 to 10,000.

Use the MS Excel to select your sample. Place 1 to 1000 in the first column. On the second column, type the formula (without the quotation marks) "=INT(10000*RAND())+1" to generate a random number. It should look like this:

Table 1: Part of a random table for sampling

Column A	Column B
1	7185
2	8706
3	8096
4	5236
5	6644
6	2035
7	4770

The numbers in column A is the sample numbering. The numbers in Column B correspond to the number of the customers in the whole population. Use these numbers to find customer #7,185, #8706 and so on. Remember, the RAND function in Excel calculates every time you open the file where you generated the random numbers. Thus, copy and drag the formula once. By the time you are done, you should have 1000 customers as a starting point.

– **Systematic Sampling**

This sampling method is used for real-time data analytics. Real-time data analytics refers to collecting sample data while the operation is ongoing. You establish a frequency to gather your sample. This frequency must be free from bias. Examples of frequencies are every fifth transaction, the first ten customers every hour and any other similar frequency. The data analyst and the management should collaborate to set the sampling frequency.

A practical example would be using systematic sampling to observe processing time. The data analyst selects five bills within an hour and measures the processing time of telephone bills. This method helps the management discover whether their customer representatives or sales account are doing their job effectively and efficiently. The management can make proactive solutions right there and then when the employees are not doing their job.

– **Stratified Random Sampling**

This method is similar to the simple random sampling strategy except for one thing. The data set is differentiated into groups. Each group must have a representative to derive a fair conclusion. The size of the sample in each group is relative to the size of the group as a whole.

For example, a loan officer wants to know the average processing time for loan applications. The lending institution has three types of loans. To create an unbiased sample, the data analyst should take samples from each type.

Table 2: A Simple Loan Dataset

Type of Loan	Loans Processed
type 1	3,000.00
type 2	4,000.00
type 3	1,000.00
Total Loans	**8,000.00**

Using the table above, the data analyst set the sample size to 5% of the total population. The sample size is 400 loans. In getting the total sample, each group will have a different sample size. Loan type 2 contributes the highest number of the sample since it has the highest number of loans processed.

Table 3 Stratified Random Sampling Computation

Type of Loan	Loans Processed	Computation	Sample Size
type 1	3,000.00	(3/8) x 400	150
type 2	4,000.00	(4/8) x 400	200
type 3	1,000.00	(1/8) x 400	50
Total Loans	**8,000.00**	**Total Sample Size**	**400**

As you can see, the sample size from Loan type 2 is 200. Using the random function in Excel, generate the sample population. Assign the population number for each type of loan. For type 1, the assigned number is 1 to 3000. For type 2, the assigned number is 1 to 4000. For type 3, the number is 1 to 1000.

You get 150 samples from loan type 1, 200 from loan type 2 and 50 from loan type 3. Use the formula =INT(####*RAND())+1, changing the number sign with the number of loans processed for each type. Use =INT(3000*RAND())+1 for loan type 1 and so on and so forth.

– Rational Subgrouping

Two basic components are important when it comes to rational subgroup sampling, the variation, and the subgroups. You measure the variation of the subgroups under the same conditions such as the duration of a shift or the quantity of output produced. The groupings help a data analyst identify the source of the variation between subgroups.

–Sample Size

The right size to represent the sample depends on two factors, the confidence level and the margin of error. The confidence level is the estimate that the analyst feels confident about the accuracy of the sample size. This level depends on how much variation does the dataset has and the total population.

Will a 5% sample size be enough when you have more than two variables? Will a 500 sample population taken from a 5M total population represents the population? These are just few of the questions you need to evaluate the confidence level of a sample size. Most of the times, determination of confidence level is a subjective one.

The margin of error is the percentage or probability that the behavior of the sample does not represent the population. The most common level of confidence is 95%, where the margin of error is 5%.

VI.   Avoiding Biases in a Data Set

Bias in data analytics refers to the errors and "impurities" within the data set being studied. You can use preventive ways in avoiding bias in a data set.

The first prevention is to create clear and specific questions in your survey that is answerable with a yes or no, or a series of options. Include a comment section if in case the answer of a respondent is not among the choices. When tabulating the survey, ensure to read the comments because these might be relevant to your research.

The second way of removing errors or biases in the dataset is the treatment of missing values. You can delete the missing values or replace it with values using the mean, median or mode. Replacement of missing values with the mean or median is called imputation.

Collect all missing values of a particular variable, get the mean or median and use the result to fill in the missing values. This type of imputation is also known as generalized imputation. Another way is same case imputation. This involves collecting missing values of each category or class. Get the mean for each category and replace the result to the missing values.

The third method of removing bias is outlier detection. Outliers are the odd-man-out kind of values in a dataset. For example, you are dealing with income of customers. In the dataset, customer's income ranges from 800,000 to 1M, annually. Out of the population, you find two or three customers with 4M and 3M income ranges.

As per data analytics principles, these customers are considered outliers because the values are significantly different from the rest of the population. The number one cause of outliers is data entry errors. Since data systems involve the intervention of users, errors are inherent during the data gathering.

You can detect outliers with histogram, and scatter plots. Techniques in removing outliers are the same with missing values. You can ignore, delete, or treat outliers as a separate group.

VII. Explaining Data

Data explanation involves the use of charts and graphs to represent your dataset. It may include the use of descriptive analysis to further back up the chart and graphs.

For example, a 2M increase in sales revenues is not sufficient for managers to formulate decisions. A data analyst should back up this data with other factors of the operation. These factors may include a 20% increase of advertisement or 15% increase in manpower. The important thing is a correlation between the other factors and the primary results.

– Descriptive analytics

Descriptive analytics describes the different components of the data in a research. This provides simple and concise summaries of a sample data and the statistical measures used. Descriptive analytics is the qualitative counterpart of a quantitative data.

Descriptive analytics is describing the "*what*" questions of the study. It presents data to the users in a convenient form because not all people can understand numerical data in percentage form or in deviation form. It helps simplify a large amount of statistical data into summaries that are more understandable.

– Charts and Graphs

Charts and graphs are data visualization tools which are used to represent your data set. These can come in the form of bar graphs, scatter plots, line graphs, and pie charts. These visualization tools are useful to some extent. These can help data analyst identify and predict values even without the use of statistical computations.

Conclusion

Data analytics is a process of data gathering, data exploration, and data explanation. Each step is essential to the success of data analytics. On top of the entire procedure is the creation of a sound study plan. Without this plan, you can never proceed systematically. The plan aids you in utilizing the resources of your company. Resources are not just limited to the financial aspect of the study. It also involves the use of data and manpower to run a research.

Chapter 4: Measures of Central Tendency

The measure of central tendency is a single value that attempts to represent a set of data. As the name implies, this value is the center of a dataset. A data analyst uses three measures of central tendency, the mean, mode, and median.

Specific uses of these measures depend on the type of variables within the dataset. One measure of central tendency may not be applicable to skewed variables while it may work in a distributed dataset.

Table 4: A simple, hypothetical sales report of a retail store

Month	Sales (in Dollars)
JANUARY	2,000.00
FEBRUARY	3,500.00
MARCH	1,000.00
APRIL	3,000.00
MAY	4,000.00
JUNE	3,000.00
JULY	2,500.00
AUGUST	1,000.00
SEPTEMBER	1,000.00
OCTOBER	2,000.00
NOVEMBER	5,000.00
DECEMBER	5,000.00

I.   Mean

The mean measure of central tendency is the average of all variables in a dataset. This is also known as the arithmetic average.

Using the table 4, you can get the mean or average by adding all the amounts and dividing it by the number of instances. The sum of the sales is 33,000. Divide it by 12 instances. You get the mean of 2,750. The equivalent function of mean in MS Excel is the "average". The arithmetic formula of mean is:

$$\bar{x} = \frac{\sum x}{n}$$

Where:
    x = is the sum of all values
    n = is the number of observances/instances/ occurrences in the data set.

This computation applies when you are dealing with the complete values of a dataset. Meaning, you are not computing a population mean. If you are working with a sample mean of a population, the formula varies slightly and the computation of sample variance is based on this computed population mean.

When to use the Mean?

Data analysts use this measure of tendency because of its simplicity and its equal representation of all the values within the dataset. The mean is applicable on continuous and discrete numerical dataset that has an even distribution. You can see an even distribution of values if the variance (or the difference) from one value to another is not far. Additionally, the graph shows a curve almost similar to a normal distribution and the values for mean, median and mode are the same.

In an extremely distorted dataset, the mean may not be a good measure of central location. Outliers and missing values can influence the behavior of the mean.
The average of all the values has the tendency to lean towards the value of the dataset that has the highest or the lowest number of occurrences. This can mislead the data analyst in the conclusion.

Other useful computations are geometric and harmonic mean. These computations are applicable in computing rate of return on investment and production costs.

II.   Distorted Distribution

To better understand this concept of extreme distortion, assume that the values in the sales report are as follows:

Table 5:
A hypothetical sales report where the months have more low sales than high ones

Month	Sales (in Dollars)
JANUARY	1,000.00
FEBRUARY	1,000.00
MARCH	1,000.00
APRIL	1,000.00
MAY	1,500.00
JUNE	3,000.00
JULY	3,000.00
AUGUST	1,000.00
SEPTEMBER	1,000.00
OCTOBER	2,000.00
NOVEMBER	3,000.00
DECEMBER	3,000.00

Computing the mean, you derive a value of 1,791.67. As you can see, the mean is lower since the highest sales in other months such as June, July, November, and December are pulled in the direction of the lowest sales. You reverse the values. The retail store has more high sales than low sales. The mean is 3,500.

Table 6:
A hypothetical sales report where the months have more high sales than low sales

Month	Sales (in Dollars)
JANUARY	5,000.00
FEBRUARY	1,000.00
MARCH	1,000.00
APRIL	1,000.00
MAY	1,000.00
JUNE	3,000.00
JULY	5,000.00
AUGUST	5,000.00
SEPTEMBER	5,000.00
OCTOBER	5,000.00
NOVEMBER	5,000.00
DECEMBER	5,000.00

III. Median

The median measure of central tendency refers to the single value between the lower half and the higher half of a dataset when you arrange the values in ascending or descending order. If the values have an odd number of occurrences, the middle of the data set is the median. If the values have an even number of observations, the median is the average of the two middle values.

For a clearer explanation, use **Table 6** in this chapter. Arrange the sales amount from lowest to highest or vice versa. Since the table has an even number of observations, there are two middle values, 2,500 and 3,000. Get the average of the two and you get the result of 2,750.

When to Use the Median?

You use the median when the dataset is skewed and the values are ordinal. You cannot use the median in a categorical dataset because the categorical values cannot assume a logical order.

To get the median of the low sales table, the median is 1,250 while the high sales median is 5,000. As you can see, the more skewed the values are, the greater is the difference between the median and mean. The values may even represent incorrectly the true pattern of the sales report.

IV. Mode

The mode counts the frequency of each variable. The value that occurs most in a dataset is the mode.

Using the same tables above, the Table 4 has the mode value of 1,000 with 3 occurrences. The mode of the Table 5 (low sales) is also 1,000 with 6 observations and the last table (high sales) has 5,000 with 7 occurrences.

When to use *Mode*?

The mode is more appropriate when used in a categorical dataset. However, there are instances that a dataset would not contain a any mode at all or that the mode does not represent the pattern of the dataset. If this is the case, the mean or median might be the applicable measurement of central location.

Sometimes, a dataset can have two or more modes. You can get the multi-modes of a dataset by clustering or grouping the variables and select each mode from the clusters. This technique may complicate the drawing of conclusions.

In an evenly distributed dataset, the mean, median and the mode values are the same. Using Table 4, the mean and median are the same but the mode varies. This might mean that the values might be distributed evenly.

V.   Variance

The variance is the difference between the values of a dataset. It is the spread of values within a set of data. A zero variance means no changes in the values are apparent. The values of the variables are all the same. The higher the value of the variance means the higher is the difference from one value to another.

– *Steps in Computing the Variance*

First, get the mean or average. Recall that the mean computed in the first part of the chapter is 2,750.

Second, use this value and subtract it with the amount of sales. Your table should look like Table 7. The squared difference is x^2. The formula for computing the variance is:

$$\sigma^2 = \frac{\sum(X - \mu)^2}{N}$$

Where:

X is the individual data values
μ is the mean of all the data (or sample population)
N is the total number of data values

Table 7: Variance Computation - Squared Difference

MONTH	SALES (IN DOLLARS)	mean	difference	Squared Difference
JANUARY	2,000.00	2750	(750.00)	562,500.00
FEBRUARY	3,500.00	2750	750.00	562,500.00
MARCH	1,000.00	2750	(1,750.00)	3,062,500.00
APRIL	3,000.00	2750	250.00	62,500.00
MAY	4,000.00	2750	1,250.00	1,562,500.00
JUNE	3,000.00	2750	250.00	62,500.00
JULY	2,500.00	2750	(250.00)	62,500.00
AUGUST	1,000.00	2750	(1,750.00)	3,062,500.00
SEPTEMBER	1,000.00	2750	(1,750.00)	3,062,500.00
OCTOBER	2,000.00	2750	(750.00)	562,500.00
NOVEMBER	5,000.00	2750	2,250.00	5,062,500.00
DECEMBER	5,000.00	2750	2,250.00	5,062,500.00

Lastly, you can compute the variance by getting the average of the squared difference. The value of the variance is 1,895,833.33.

When dealing with a sample variance, the denominator is N – 1. This prevents bias on the computed variance.

VI.   Standard Deviation

After computing the variance, you can get the standard deviation by getting the square root of the sum of squared difference. The formula is simple.

$\sqrt{1,895,833.33}$ is 1,377, rounded to the nearest number.

What is the use of standard deviation?

The standard deviation tells the data analyst the dispersion of the data from the mean or median. It tells how far or how near is a variable to the mean or the median. Standard deviation alone is not sufficient to establish the behavior of variables within the data set. You have to consider other measures to come up with a meaningful interpretation.

VII.   Coefficient of Variation

This is the ratio of the standard deviation to the mean and the formula to compute the coefficient is:

Coefficient of Variation = (Standard Deviation / Mean) * 100.

Continuing with the given example of this chapter, the computation is as follows:

CV = (1,377 / 2,750) * 100%
CV = 50.07%

VIII. Drawing Conclusions

Interpreting the results of the statistical computations is important in data analytics. Numbers alone are useless to the data analyst. Although data interpretation is sometimes subjective, you can use the standard way of interpreting the different statistical measures of central tendency.

Mean, median and mode are the center location of a dataset. Mean is the average of all data values. Using the examples in this chapter, you can assume that every year the average sale of the retail industry is 2,750. However, this conclusion alone is not enough. Combine the mean with standard deviation, the results and interpretation become meaningful. The standard deviation in the example is 1,377. This means that the sales of the retail store can either go down or go up in the amount of 1,377.

The coefficient of variation indicates the percentage of variance within the values of a dataset. It shows how much does a certain value may deviate from the mean. It is basically similar to standard deviation. Interpreting the results, the retail stores can have a sales 50% higher or lower than the mean of 2,750.

The variance result is not a stand-alone value. You cannot derive any conclusion from this value except for computation purposes. You compute variance so you can proceed with standard deviation and coefficient of variation.

Conclusion

Mean, mode and median are great measurements of central tendency but to interpret the behavior or patterns in a dataset, you need to compute for the standard deviation or coefficient of variance. These measurements tell you how varied a value can be within the dataset.

Chapter 5: Charts and Graphs

Data visualization is an essential tool when it comes to representing the results of data analytics. In conveying the results, accuracy is important along with choosing the right data visuals. You can use pie charts, bar graphs or X-Y graphs.

I.   Pie Charts

The most common chart used for this purpose would be the pie graph. Despite its simplicity, many users do not know how to interpret results based on what a pie chart represents. Furthermore, data analytics experts argue that a pie graph is the most useless data representation a data analyst can use. Criticisms aside, a pie chart has its own merit and limitations.

–   The Basics

A pie chart is excellent for data representation if you are working with 6 or less variables as the result of data analytics. Six slices in the pie chart make the visual easy to read and interpret. Each slice of the pie chart represents a part of a whole.

You can use a pie chart for nominal and numeric data. As long as the variables do not exceed 6, you can use a pie chart to represent the variables. Another requirement of using a pie chart is a dramatic change among the variables. This means the variance between variables is evident.

Example with Illustration

You are working with a sample dataset of a call center with more than 200,000 call transactions starting from January 2015 to January 2016. The variables (column heading) of the dataset are as follows:

Customer Country /Region	Issue Code 1	Service Request Id	Support Center Filter	Support Channel	Ticket Close Date	Ticket Create Date	Vendor - Site	Time To Close

The management wants to know the most common support channel that customers use to reach the call center. Based on the data given to you, customers use three communication channels to reach the call center. These channels are e-mail, inbound call, and chat. Use a pie chart to represent the number of transactions in each channel.

58% of the customers from more than 200,000 call transactions are using the **CHAT** to file complaints, place an order, pay their bills or make any other transactions. Based on the pie chart, customers find it more convenient to make transactions using the chat channel because of its interactive feature. Customers can ask questions immediately without waiting for hours as compared with email.

You can use the pie chart to formulate decisions. However, to create an effective decision, the results you see in a pie chart alone are not enough. You will need to make further data exploration.

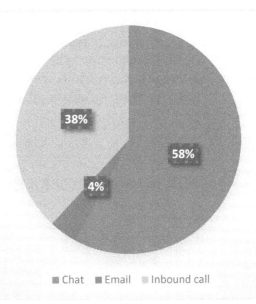

Figure 1 Pie chart of a call center using 3 communication channels

– **Limitations of Pie chart**

One notable limitation is the use of variables. A pie chart is more readable when you are working with 6 or fewer variables. Any number more than 6 variables will make a pie chart a poor choice of data visualization.

The second limitation is the use of visual representation. Without any legends on the pie graph, reading can be hard for some. It may even create confusion if the differences between variables are not significant. You need to use light to dark colors to properly separate and represent your variables. In some cases, especially if there are more than 6 variables, a pie chart turns into a wheel of colors. It may be attractive to look at but the purpose of representing data is rendered useless

Refer to the pie chart of a hypothetical sales report of a retail store. As you can see, the distribution is not drastic, making the pie chart not a good choice for this kind of data set. Furthermore, the variables are more than 6. In this pie chart of a hypothetical sales report, the sales report consists of 12 months. The best visual representation of this type of data set is a bar graph.

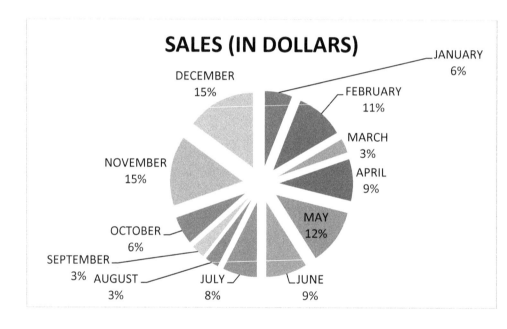

SALES (IN DOLLARS)

JANUARY 6%
FEBRUARY 11%
MARCH 3%
APRIL 9%
MAY 12%
JUNE 9%
JULY 8%
AUGUST 3%
SEPTEMBER 3%
OCTOBER 6%
NOVEMBER 15%
DECEMBER 15%

Figure 2 Pie chart of a hypothetical sales report (see tables in chapter 4)

A pie chart is an excellent data visualization if you use it correctly. For optimum readability, arrange your figures in a clockwise orientation. Use 2-D presentation. Three dimensional pie charts may look creative but sometimes, the results are somewhat distorted.

If you are working with more than 6 variables, use other visualization to represent your results. One thing you should always avoid in communicating data insights is that people misunderstand your results. Any misunderstanding yields more cost on the part of the business.

Creating a Pie Chart in MS Excel

With computer and MS Excel, creating a pie graph is easy. In this section, learn how to create a simple pie chart. Using the example of the call center company, arrange your data into this order in a spreadsheet.

Communication Channel	Number of Calls per Channel
Chat	126,580.00
Email	8,817.00
Inbound call	83,271.00

1. The communication channel should be in the first column (A column) and the number of calls per channel is in the second column (B column).

2. Highlight the cell range. Click "Insert" and select Pie Chart in the option. Select the 2-D orientation. 3D may look better than 2D but 3D orientation distorts data distribution.

3. You can format the style of the chart. In MS Excel 2013 edition, more chart styles are available. In the example (call center company), the style shows the percentage of each channel. You can also display the numerical figures inside the graph as labels. See Figure 1.

II.   Bar Graphs

Like the pie chart, a bar graph is a data visualization tool—but this one uses bars and the X-Y axis to represent and compare data. The orientation can be horizontal or vertical. In this tool, the longer the bar is (or higher in the case of vertical orientation) the higher is the value of data.

The categories or independent variables are always located on the x-axis (horizontal) while the numeric values are on the y-axis (vertical). You can use the categories as labels of to the X and Y axes or use them as legends.

One advantage of a bar graph is its flexibility. You can compare many categories with many attributes and still achieve readability. A user can interpret a bar graph at a glance.

Example of a Bar Graph

Using the hypothetical sales report used in chapter 4, assume that the first set of values is the sales for the year 2014. You obtain the sales report for 2015 and 2016.

Table 8: Hypothetical Sales Report for 2014, 2015, 2016

MONTH	Year 2014	Year 2015	Year 2016
JANUARY	2,000.00	1,500.00	2,500.00
FEBRUARY	3,500.00	3,000.00	3,700.00
MARCH	1,000.00	1,500.00	1,000.00
APRIL	3,000.00	3,500.00	3,200.00
MAY	4,000.00	3,800.00	4,200.00
JUNE	3,000.00	3,200.00	3,200.00
JULY	2,500.00	2,700.00	2,900.00

AUGUST	1,000.00	1,000.00	1,500.00
SEPTEMBER	1,000.00	1,100.00	1,200.00
OCTOBER	2,000.00	2,500.00	2,600.00
NOVEMBER	5,000.00	5,000.00	5,000.00
DECEMBER	5,000.00	5,200.00	5,300.00

The Bar graph looks like the figure using the assumed values in Table 8.

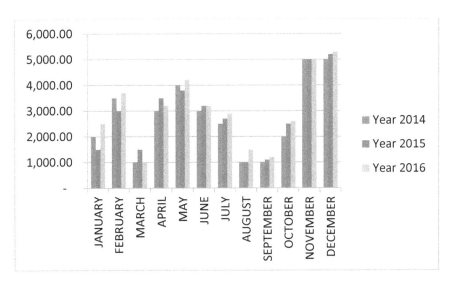

Figure 3 Bar graph for 2014, 2015, 2016

Looking at the bar graph in Figure 3, you can say that the month of December for each year has the highest sales while the month of March and August has the lowest sales for 2 years.

The bar graph example cannot show anything more than the values and a few categories. Thus, you need to supplement your data visualization tools with descriptive analytics. Alternatively, break down the monthly sales report and show the factors that affect the sales for each month.

Create a Bar Graph in MS Excel

The procedures of creating a bar graph in MS Excel is almost similar to pie chart creation except when choosing the style of chart or graph.

1. First, highlight the dataset in Excel. Click Insert and select the Column or Bar chart. The column style is the traditional bar chart, where the independent variable is in the X-axis and the dependent variable is in the Y-axis. The Bar Chart is the horizontal bar graph, wherein the values are represented horizontally.

2. Horizontal bar charts are useful when the labels of the independent variables are too long and reading the data interpretations is more convenient horizontally than with a column chart. An example of the column style is Figure 3.

3. In MS Excel 2013 edition, a combo chart is available. This style combines the line chart and a bar graph.

III. Time Charts and Line Graphs

Line graphs are almost similar to a bar graph, except this one makes use of use lines instead of bars to represent the data. You use a line graph when you aim to show changes of values over time. The independent variables are placed on the X-axis. Using the hypothetical sales report, the month is placed on the X-axis.

If you want to compare the sales between years and you like to see which year is the most profitable, line graph is the best option. Although you can make the same conclusion with a bar graph, the line graph is preferable since you can see the trend of the sales every year at a glance.

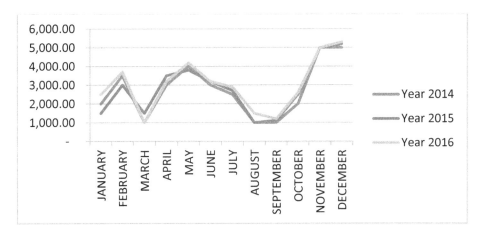

Figure 4 Line graph for a hypothetical sales report

With the line graph, you would be able to properly show that the distinctions between the years are very slight. The sales for the year 2016 are generally higher than the previous two years. The universal users of this data visualization are finance, marketing, and other industries that want to compare values based on elapsed time.

A line graph is sometimes called the time chart because analyst uses time as the primary variable for it.

Create Time Charts and Line Graphs in MS Excel

1. Copy the values in Table 8. Highlight the columns and rows. Click Insert then select Line. If you choose the 2-D orientation, MS Excel creates a line graph similar to

Figure 4. You can change the location of the legends or opt to remove them and place it as a label for each line.

IV.   Histograms

The presentation of a histogram is similar to a bar graph, except that you designate a range or "bins" for the continuous variables. Histograms show the dispersion of a data set. To create an effective histogram, the key is to identify the correct bins. You interpret the data based on the area of the bars, which is a major difference from the bar graph.

Too many bins result to the bars being too small, making it hard for the user to see the correlation between the variables. Too few bins yield bars that are too wide, creating an incorrect correlation between the variables. This forfeits the purpose of the histogram. Bins that are identified correctly can show the dispersion of a data.

Create Histograms in MS Excel

The version of this step-by-step creation of histogram is MS Excel 2010. Other versions starting 2007 work the same so you can still use this to activate and create histograms in MS Excel. However, versions earlier than 2007 may have slightly different locations for the items described in this tutorial but the labels are still similar.

1. First, activate the Excel Add-ins in your PC. By default, it is disabled. Open the File tab and click the Options.

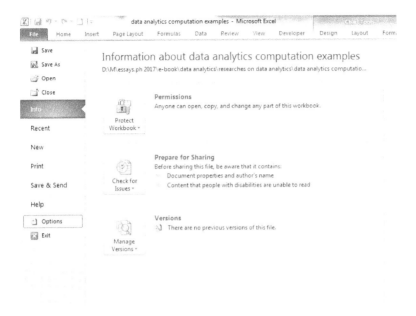

2. Choose Add-ins. Highlight the Analysis ToolPak. In the bottom part of the window, select Excel Add-ins and click Go.

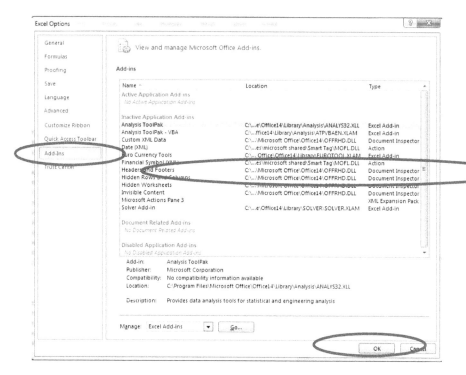

3. Check Analysis ToolPak and click Ok.

4. After you're done, the Data tab in Excel should show an additional option "Data Analysis."

5. Encode the data set in Excel. One column contains the numeric values and another one consists of the bin (or range) of the values.

6. Highlight the dataset, and click on the Data Analysis on the Data tab. A window selection would appear. Select Histogram and click on OK.

7. The histogram creation window appears. It will require you to select input range and bin range. The input range is the data cell range where you encode the numeric values. For the bin range, select the column where you place the bins. Remember to check the chart output. If you want, you can also specify the output range. The

output can be in the same worksheet, another worksheet or another workbook.

V.   Scatter Plots

Also known as the X-Y graph, the use of a scatter plot is applicable for a data set with two or more correlated variables. Scatter graph is effective if you are working with numeric variables. These variables are always in pairs, wherein pair 1 affects the occurrence of pair 2 or pair 1 and pair 2 affects the occurrence of another factor.

For example, a retail store manager suspects that there are two characteristics of a product that influences the buying behavior of an individual. Using a scatter graph, the analyst plots these values on the scatter graph to see if there is really a correlation between the characteristics of the product and the purchasing behavior of customers.

If a correlation exists, the plot points should be placed close together enough to see a distinct regression line of the points. If the theory is somehow false, the points are scattered. However, you should not stop here.

To determine the accuracy of the scatter graph, supplement the visualization tool with statistical computation. If your computation results to a no-correlation value then, there is no correlation between the variables. It might happen that despite the distinct regression line in the scatter graph, there is no correlation between the variables at all. It could happen that the correlated points are created in random.

Create Scatter Plots in MS Excel

1. You will need pairs of data. Each pair represents the X and Y axes. The X axis consists of the independent variables and Y is the dependent variables

2. First, arrange your dataset. The first column is the independent variable and the second column composes of your dependent variables.

3. Highlight the dataset, click Insert tab and select the Scatter chart in the options. The graph should look like this:

Figure 5: A simple scatter plot

As you can see, the points are minimal since the sample data set contains few values and variables. A scatter plot like this is a little difficult to interpret due to the lack of a visible regression line. However, if you are dealing with thousands of data with two or more variables, the points are either scattered or closely gathered in the center or near the regression line. It will resemble stars in the sky at night, where points are close or far from one another.

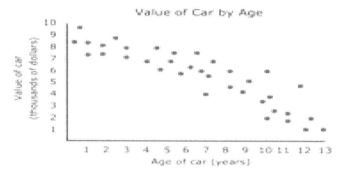

Figure 6: Another example of Scatter plots

You can see a distinct regression line wherein the value of car diminishes as the car ages. If you are to get the value of car when it reaches the age of 3 years, you can see the points of 7,000 to 8,000.

VI.   Spatial Plot and Map

This visualization tool is specific to data analytics that uses the R program. This tool is a way of representing underlying relationships through spatial analysis. A spatial analysis is most useful in the health institutions, pharmaceutical, and public sector. The data analyst can use data from a population who buys medicines and their addresses to plot what kinds of diseases are being treated in the area.

Health institutions can use spatial maps to discover outbreak in a region and establish necessary precautions to prevent the disease from spreading. This kind of map is also useful to pharmaceutical companies in developing the cure for the disease using the data gathered in a spatial analysis.

Conclusion

The different charts and graphs are important in data insight communications. However, the effectiveness of these charts and graphs depends on the type of data you are presenting. A certain chart may not be applicable to nominal data while another one may represent the data effectively. Supplement these charts and graphs with descriptive analytics to make interpretation more understandable.

Chapter 6: Applying Data Analytics to Business and Industry

Business Intelligence (BI) is a business software solution. It collects data and integrates statistical techniques in analyzing data, deriving, and presenting data insights to the business management for improving business operations. The application of Business Intelligence is to support the decision making a process of a business. Business Intelligence system provides data-driven decisions.

I.   Importance of Business Intelligence

Business Intelligence provides current and predictive views of business operations. These views are generated by using data from data mart and working with operational data. The features of a BI software support different reporting applications, pivot-table analyses with interactive slicing and dicing of data sets, visualization tools, and statistical data gathering techniques. BI applications include gathering sales, marketing, production, nonfinancial, financial, and other data sources. Information involves benchmarking where data from other companies are compiled and analyzed.

II.   The Goals of Business Intelligence

The true worth of data is not inherent. Its true value is derived from effectively using it for practical purposes. The changes that businesses make based on provided data insights define the worth of a data as well as the means of gathering it. When a BI analyst explores data and calculates return on investment on business reports, the calculation is based on the use of the product.

The goal of business intelligence is to help the management make effective decisions that the front liners can use when it comes to dealing with different customer inquiries, as well as for addressing customer complaints and explaining new products to customers. Business intelligence helps a business runs the business. It helps them make real-time decisions to avoid delays.

III.   How can data analyst benefit from the use of a BI?

The data analyst can use BI to help boost the performance of an operation or a system network of a small business to a multimillion dollar company. Aside from this, an analyst can use BI to evaluate the accuracy of a study. BI automates the process of data analytics without having to go through studying different programming languages to create models. This is a great leap in both speed in accuracy compared to doing things manually.

Business Intelligence would also helps adata analyst formulate actionable information. With data being accessed real-time, a data analyst can make a real-time forecast on sales, marketing, and financial information. Since the data sets are real time, the data analyst can provide speedy answers to management. The managers do not need to wait for days. Speedy answers mean fast decision making. Fast decision making means increased customer satisfaction.

IV. Data Analytics in Business and Industry

Data analytics has come a long way since it was first put into use by different businesses. These days, an average data analyst would exposed to the different types of online and real-time data which they must learn to familiarize themselves with.

Here are a few examples:

– Transactional Data

Transactional data is recorded from transactions. A transaction, then, is the exchange of information in a sequential manner that involves completing a request. An example of transactional data is a customer purchase made in a retail store. Transactional data can be logistics, job-related or financial in nature. It includes the time, who processed the transaction, the type of transaction, who recorded the transaction and other relevant references.

– Social Data

Social data refers to online data that involves public and private information about an individual. Since the appearance of social media networks, information about different individuals and market segments have become more accessible online.

To some extent, social data is more credible than survey data. Since people use this data for sharing important information to other people, data on personal information is more accurate than information from an online survey. Additionally, social data helps a business gather real-time reactions to its service or products.

– Machine Data from Business Operations

This refers to raw data from software solutions. Machine data includes behavior from mobile users who connect to the business network. Examples of machine data are applications, call data records, business information system logs and customer's online connection through a business e-commerce site.

A business network, however, is prone to errors and failure due to constant heavy usage or another user hacking the system. Errors in the system, performance of the software and other relative issues with maintaining an information system are important in machine data analytics.

With this dataset (system performance), different people in a business can evaluate the overall performance of the software, and improve security features of the network

V.   The Different Business Intelligence Solutions

Big companies who have been using data analytics and business intelligence also offers BI solutions. Some of these solutions include the BI software provided by IBM and Microsoft. This software is available through on-premise and through cloud computing platform.

On-premise business intelligence solutions involves the installation of the software on company networks and computer hardware. It may include a dedicated server that the company is willing to set-up in order to run a more comprehensive business intelligence system.

The newest business intelligence solutions also make use of cloud computing platforms. For this, the company has to register with a cloud computing entity. The bulk of maintenance lies on the company that offers the cloud platform. Despite this fact, the company or business still owns the right to the business intelligence solutions.

The advantage of on-premise BI solution is the fact that the company would have complete control of the system. The business would have the option to enhance its security features and improve the usage of the business solutions using machine data analytics. One disadvantage is the update issues. It would need to be updated in order for the BI to fully utilize new features and apply these features to your data analytics and business intelligence processes.

Another advantage is the interactive feature of BI solutions. A data analyst can access and update data information on a real-time basis. This real-time update is a big plus for businesses that rely on real-time decision making. Some examples of such businesses are an e-commerce site, telecommunications industry, banks and other financial institutions. Gaming and travel industry are also benefiting from the use of business intelligence solutions.

One argument regarding cloud computing platform is the issues on security. Since your database is managed off-site (meaning outside the premises of your company), you do not have any control over any security and safety issues. Although you can file a complaint against the cloud computing company, data breach may cost millions in lost sales or revenues.

VI. Business insights with Business Intelligence

One important business insight provided by business intelligence would be its ability to predict the needs of individual customers and profitability of products or investments. This information from the company BI is important when it comes to determining the type of products for cross-selling. This is very important to the retail industry.

With business intelligence, managers of retail stores can instruct the sales department to sell a certain product with another product (or cross-selling). Coupled with promotional content or discount, the insight may increase the sales of the retail store.

Business intelligence gives the data analyst and management a predictive power by analyzing real-time data. By analyzing and observing the ongoing transactions of a business, you can predict what customers want with a product or services. Use this data to create a promotional campaign for next week or next month.

Business insights derived from business intelligence broadens a data analyst's and a manager's perspective. With business intelligence processes, you do not limit yourself to a particular dataset. If you need a broader scope of the study to determine what brings a certain behavior, business intelligence can bring you the necessary dataset to complete the study.

VII. Business Intelligence Processes

The processes used by a BI to come up with insights includes: market analysis, competitive analysis, and SWOT analysis.

Market analysis is determining the characteristics of your market and how your market behaves when you introduce a new product or services. This analysis involves specific targeting of potential customers while maintaining loyalty from your existing customers. This involves external and internal data sources for the study. You can use surveys or experimentation.

Competitive analysis involves studying your competitors and how are they performing in the industry. It is also called benchmarking. A competitive analysis involves market identification, a definition of strength and weaknesses. You will need external data sources to complete this study.

SWOT analysis is the study of strength and weaknesses, opportunities, and threats of the business. This is an entirely internal in nature. Although at some point of the study (such as the threats identification), you will need external data sources to make comparisons. The SWOT analysis helps business improve performance and identify opportunities that the business can exploit to become competitive in its industry.

VIII. Multidimensional Database and its Benefits

The multidimensional database presents a higher level of data organization. It enhances data visualization and navigation. Maintenance is comparably lower in cost and data processing performance increases.

The graphical representation of a multidimensional database is a cube. Each variable in a data set is represented by a cube. When data is updated into the system, the system automatically looks for the particular cube that a certain type of datum belongs to. Multidimensional databases also work faster than relational databases.

– OLAP and its uses

On-Line Analytical Processing technique helps the data analyst when it comes to dealing with multidimensional databases. Using OLAP in data analytics greatly aids a data analyst in analyzing a large set of databases with multi-variables.

It enables the analysts and managers to properly develop virtual comparisons and illustrations of data insights from a multidimensional database. It is mostly comes as a feature of Business Intelligence solutions. The common uses of OLAP are specifically meant for: marketing, sales, and financial management reports of a business. It also includes business and management performance evaluation. OLAP involves financial reporting and forecasting. Despite the name, the OLAP is not always online.

OLAP has two major activities:

- The first activity is the identification of the different attributes or dimensions that are considered as "target values". These dimensions classify items into independent values while target attributes are entries in a multidimensional database and are classified as continuous variables.

- The second activity is finding the values of the entries in the multidimensional database by summing up the values of target attributes.

OLAP also has three types, MOLAP, ROLAP, and HOLAP.

- Multidimensional OLAP (MOLAP) is the typical form of the OLAP. It uses product codes, time intervals, and other similar demographic categories.

- Relational OLAP (ROLAP) entails interrelationship between attributes.

- Hybrid OLAP (HOLAP) is the combination of MOLAP and ROLAP.

OLAP is comprised of 6 different phases.

- The first phase is creating the hypercube. The hypercube is an extension of the multidimensional database.

- The second phase is slicing. Slicing involves picking a range of cells from the hypercube through identifying at least one element of the database.

- Dicing is selecting the cells and specifying a collection of attributes. It involves slicing more than two elements or dimensions.

- Roll up refers to computing the sum of the values from one or more dimensions. An example is computing the sum of the sales for five years.

- Drill down and up means splitting an attribute by detailing (drill down) or summarizing (drill up). For example, you split the sales data by yearly sales into monthly totals, from monthly sales to daily totals or from daily totals to a per hour basis.

– Pivot is altering the orientation of a report.

What is Data Mart?

A ***data mart*** is a subgroup of a data warehouse. It is specific to a particular department or line of business within an organization. A data mart is a small scale multidimensional network. Its components are software, computer and network hardware and data that belong to the department.

One characteristic of data mart is the isolation of use, improvement and management of data. Data in this setting is read only. This improves response time for the end users of the department. Data mart also allows users to access the specific data that is constantly used.

Businesses, especially large ones, build data marts due to help them in handling the disorganized manner many (if not all) big databases handle information. Most of the times, database administrator has to build complex queries so that users from every department can access data they need.

A ***Data warehouse*** is different from a data mart, although a data mart contains all the necessary components of a data warehouse except that the setting is more condensed. Data warehouses would often have a number of subject areas while data mart focuses on one area or a specific department. Data warehouse holds comprehensive information while data mart contains summarized data.

Businesses create data marts because of the easy access it provides end users, especially when it comes to data that is frequently needed. Creation and implementation is easier and faster compared to a full data warehouse. Businesses can easily identify users. Since businesses can identify the users of data mart, they can enhance user's experience and observe how users access and exploit data in the operation.

IX.   BI and Data Analytics

Data analytics is also part of business intelligence. The difference and similarities between the two are often indistinguishable. Most of the time, data analytics is incorporated in business intelligence. Data analytics and business intelligence may seem two different fields in analyzing data, depending on a person's point of view. Some people say data analytics is the business intelligence. Others argue that business intelligence is a separate field from data analytics.

– Similarities
Analytics and business intelligence involve analyzing data to come up with useful information for business use. Both include the use of statistical methods and computations to derive results. Analytics and business intelligence also uses a complex programming language to hasten the process of computation.

– Distinctions
One major distinction between analytics and BI is the way data is used. Analytics mostly deals with historical data while BI involves access to real-time information. Business needs BI to run essential operations while data analytics focuses on improving the operations of the business.

Another distinction is the cost of investment. Business intelligence solutions are way more expensive than data analytics because BI is a software solution while data analytics is a method.

Whatever the purpose a user has when it comes to utilizing data analytics and business intelligence, these two are known essentials in any business. Small scale businesses can use data analytics to improve their operations while large corporations can use business intelligence and data analytics to become more competitive.

In Closing

Data analytics has many uses in the business, government and education sectors. Throughout the years, it has helped plenty of companies when it comes to dealing with problems in operations, in enhancing customer services and in providing innovative products. In the government sector, data analytics is a big help in maintaining national security and public welfare while the education sector has used data analytics to improve the quality of education.

Despite its advantages, many organizations, both big and small, in the private sector do not know how to harness the power of data analytics. Many of these organizations do not utilize or maximize the benefits that it can provide them with, especially when it comes to making better informed decisions for the improvement of their overall operations.

Data analytics is not just the work of a single data analyst. This is the combined effort of the management, data analyst, and project sponsor. In a larger scale, project managers, database administrator and data engineer have key roles in the success of data analytics.

The role of the management in data analytics is important since they are the ones who have the power to specify the objectives of the study. The objective which must clearly be communicated with the data analyst. At the same, the data analyst has to communicate his/her concerns or any conflict to the management. Conflicts that can be encountered may include the acquisition of data sources or setting a deadline. External forces such as competitors are also important in balancing the equation.

In this world where data resources are abundant and competition is fierce, a data analyst and management must work closely together to achieve competitive advantage. Unity, proper planning and communication are the keys of a successful data analytics. Despite external forces that may discourage a business, these keys to success will help any business achieve whatever goals it wants, either the goals are short-term or long-term in nature.

Conclusion

Thank you again for purchasing this book, I hope you enjoyed reading it as much as I enjoyed writing it for you!

Finally, if you enjoyed this book I'd like to ask you to leave a review for my book on Amazon, it would be greatly appreciated!

All the best and good luck.

www.ingramcontent.com/pod-product-compliance
Lightning Source LLC
LaVergne TN
LVHW052310060326
832902LV00021B/3796